D1537527

Published by Resurgence Publishing ™

Resurgence Publishing, LLC. 1411 NW 50th Street, Seattle, WA 98107, U.S.A.

First published in 2012 by Resurgence

Printed in the United States of America

ISBN-13: 978-1-938805-00-4
ISBN-10: 1938805003

# RESURGENCE®

## GET TRAINED

## THIS IS A RESURGENCE BOOK.

It's a book to help train you for life and ministry as a Christian. The Resurgence exists to train people to love Jesus and live a life of worship.

## WE DO THIS THROUGH:

**theresurgence.com** – The most-visited Christian-training blog online
**Resurgence Events** – The latest events can be found on theresurgence.com
**Resurgence Training Center** – A masters-level theology program
**Resurgence Books** – A line of books like this one

Find out more at **theresurgence.com**.

# TABLE OF CONTENTS

# ABOUT THIS GUIDE

## WHY YOU NEED THIS GUIDE

This study has been designed to help you and your community group experience the transforming power of the gospel through life together on mission with Jesus. Use this guide as simply that, a guide. As you work through these materials, be open to what God is calling you to as a community group leader and disciple.

## HOW TO USE THIS GUIDE

Before you gather each week, read the corresponding chapter in *Community: Taking Your Small Group Off Life Support*, and review the section introduction. When you gather together, start with the Scripture reflection, and then launch into group discussion and prayer.

## BUT WAIT, THERE'S MORE

Use the time between your group gatherings to prayerfully consider how God demonstrates to you the power of the gospel in the context of community groups. Then communicate to your group your personal reflections and what you've learned, and be mindful of how to continue bearing fruit as a community group leader.

## PREPARATION

Pray. Pray that your heart would be open to hearing God's call for you as a leader within your community. God may reveal things to you that you did not previously consider; this is a time to humbly embrace God's truth in your life. Pray for the conversations you will have with your community group members, and pray for their hearts as well. Pray that God would speak clearly through the materials and group discussion. Pray that this experience of learning and growing would be faith-driven, fun, and fruitful.

## READ

You want your community to be impacted, and the best way to make use of your time is to be prepared beforehand. Have your group members read the corresponding chapter in *Community: Taking Your Small Group Off Life Support* before your community group gathers to discuss the material.

## IT'S ALL ABOUT JESUS

Nothing in your community group is as important as the person and work of Jesus and being a community that enjoys his goodness, together. Jesus' life, death, and resurrection make it possible for us to even be in community together. God is glorified when we come together to pursue him. So delight in God's glory as you work through this guide together.

## DIAGNOSTIC

Appendix 4 is a survey to assess the health of your community group. If you are using this study to "re-launch" your group, then use the assessment before you go through this workbook. That way, you'll be able to make first things first by setting benchmarks for your community's health. After you complete the survey, revisit this tool every six months or so to mark your progress. If you are launching a new group, use this tool every six months and have each member fill out the survey. That way, leaders will get a fair assessment of the health of the group.

# INTRODUCTION

Developing a community group from the ground up can seem impossible. Many of us have had small group experiences that are old and stale. These groups are often socially awkward, and attending them week after week feels more like a chore than the life-giving experience that it could be. Or maybe we have no experience with real community and don't even know where to start.

The goal of this series is to examine what it means to live out our faith in community in a way that bears fruit in our own backyards and glorifies the name of Jesus. This may require some rethinking of what it means to be a community group. I want to give you permission throughout this series to shake the Etch A Sketch of small groups and find the freedom to reimagine life in community. Challenge yourself to realize that community is a gift from God to support us during life's trials, sustain us during life's triumphs, and seek him as we live out his will here on earth.

# SESSION 1:
## THE FOUNDATION

*From chapters 1 and 2 of* Community: Taking Your Small Group Off Life Support:

## THE *WHY* OF COMMUNITY

Before we ask *how* to do community, we must ask ourselves *why* we do community. If we don't have a clear understanding of why we are in community in the first place, our groups will be lifeless. Growth, retention, belonging, and health are important byproducts of community, but they are just that: byproducts. We cannot take the good fruit of healthy, gospel-saturated community and make it the purpose.

The foundational reason (the *why*) for church community is to image God and proclaim the good news of what Jesus has accomplished on the cross. *"Community is for us a declaration of the overwhelming love of God, a tangible proclamation of the reconciling work of the cross.* This is a truly compelling reason to build community groups within our churches. This is the bigger purpose that can inspire real community. Community groups are a living illustration of the gospel and its power to save. The world needs this, and so does your church."[1]

## COMMUNITY IS NOT OPTIONAL

"Community groups are essential to the Christian life because we were created for community. We were built to function in relationship with one another and with God. We are able to do so through the grace and reconciliation made possible by the death and resurrection of Jesus. Community, therefore, is an expression of who God is in Trinitarian relationship and a testimony to his love in redeeming us as a people through Jesus.

---

[1] Brad House, *Community: Taking Your Small Group Off Life Support* (Wheaton, IL: Crossway, 2011), 34.

"We must conclude that if God created community for this purpose, it should be an essential part of every Christian's life. The marginalization of community within the church and culture has not come from conviction but from apathy and isolation brought on by sin. Isolation is our response to sin. Community is our response to reconciliation.

"When we don't ask why we have community, it becomes a secondary function of the church rather than the primary vehicle through which God moves and makes his glory known. To resuscitate life in the community of God, we must reestablish the foundational purpose of community. We must root it in the cross.

"If we want to take our small group communities off life support, we need to go to the source. We need the atoning work of Jesus that brings the dead to life. It is the gospel that plucked us from death, and it is the gospel that will breathe life into our anemic communities.

"The inspiration for community is the death and resurrection of Jesus. It is the glimpse of his glorious return. It is the power over sin. It is his victory over death. As we receive the gift of grace and believe in the promise of what Jesus accomplished, we are compelled by the grace of our Savior to proclaim this great act of love. Living grace-filled lives in a community marked by humility and love, which seeks to reconcile one to another and broken lives to God, is the perfect means for such a proclamation.

"We do not have community groups to close the back door of the church. We do not have groups because people need to belong or we need to care for one another. These are good but secondary effects of authentic community. These effects are not the foundation. We have community groups because we have seen the glory of God and we have been given the grace to live our lives to exalt the Christ. We have community groups because we have been reconciled to God and one another. We once were not a people but now we are a people of God's own possession. We have community groups as a proclamation of the goodness of our God and testimony to the completed work of the cross. This is the foundation for gospel-saturated community that will overflow with life."[2]

---

2  House, *Community*, 42–43.

## 1.1 Scripture Reflection

Ephesians 2:15b–22: "[15]. . . that he might create in himself one new man in place of the two, so making peace, [16]and might reconcile us both to God in one body through the cross, thereby killing the hostility. [17]And he came and preached peace to you who were far off and peace to those who were near. [18]For through him we both have access in one Spirit to the Father. [19]So then you are no longer strangers and aliens, but you are fellow citizens with the saints and members of the household of God, [20]built on the foundation of the apostles and prophets, Christ Jesus himself being the cornerstone, [21]in whom the whole structure, being joined together, grows into a holy temple in the Lord. [22]In him you also are being built together into a dwelling place for God by the Spirit."

_____

_____

_____

## 1.2 Group Discussion

1.   What assumption have we made about what it means to be a member of a community group?

_____

_____

_____

2.   How does the purpose of community groups affect how we experience community?

_____

_____

_____

3. List the reasons you have heard or used to encourage participation in community (start with the assumption from question 1). Now put each into one of three categories:

- Reason: WHY we live out our faith in community rooted in what Jesus has done

_____

_____

_____

- Practice: WHAT we do as a community

_____

_____

_____

- Purpose: the FOR or the fruit of gospel-centered community

_____

_____

_____

4. What are the pitfalls of building community on a foundation of practice or purpose?

_____

_____

_____

5. Why is it important that we see the image of God and the reconciliation of Jesus as the foundation for our community?

_____

_____

_____

6.  What are the internal obstacles to creating an environment of discipleship, care, and mission within our community?

_____

_____

_____

## 1.3 Prayer

• Pray this week asking the Holy Spirit to help us grow together as a community that reflects the power of the cross.
• Pray that we would identify the barriers in our hearts that inhibit life-giving community.
• Pray that we begin to experience life-giving community with one another.

## 1.4 Experience

If we are going to be a group on mission that can listen to others' stories and point them to Christ, we must first start with learning each other's story. Take the time to share how God has brought each of you into his story. You can do this in one sitting, or you may want to have one or two people share their story at the beginning of each session for the next six weeks.

## 1.5 Personal Reflection

As previously mentioned, the purpose of community is to declare the goodness of God and to proclaim the gospel. How does this understanding change the way you look at your participation in community?

_____

_____

_____

_____

# SESSION 2:
# OWNERSHIP

*From chapter 3 of* Community: Taking Your Small Group Off Life Support:

## COMMUNITY OWNERSHIP

The goal of this lesson is to wrestle with the question, Does our community own the mission of God for our church, or do we just agree with it?

"Agreement simply means that people like the idea of the mission and are excited about someone at the church carrying it out. They may not, and probably don't, see themselves as the church, or at least not the part of the church that lives out the mission. This manifests in casual attendance and participation in programs and events that serve their needs but don't require anything of them. Agreement can even involve serving in various ministries if the bar is low enough; but if the mission is not owned, if it is not internalized within the people, then they will not take risks for the sake of the gospel. They won't risk comfort, time, money, or self-interest for the mission to see Jesus glorified.

"Our churches are filled with people who agree with the mission but do not own it. Ownership is marked by joy-filled sacrifice that sees kingdom work as a 'get to' because of what Christ has done, rather than a 'got to' out of Christian duty. Ownership looks like people serving the church and the city with a passion for the gospel. It looks like people cheerfully and sacrificially giving out of love for Jesus to see the work of the gospel move forward. Ownership looks like people participating in the messiness of community and being inconvenienced for the sake of another's sanctification."[1]

"If we want to be a missional church that sees the lives in our cities transformed by the gospel, we must foster a holy discontentment with the status quo and resist apathy toward God's mission. Compelled by the grace of

---

[1]   House, *Community*, 72–73.

God manifested in the atoning work of Jesus on the cross and his resurrection, we can take ownership of proclaiming the truth of the gospel and living it out in community."[2]

---

2  Ibid., 81.

## 2.1 Scripture Reflection

2 Corinthians 5:17–6:1: "[17]Therefore, if anyone is in Christ, he is a new creation. The old has passed away; behold, the new has come. [18]All this is from God, who through Christ reconciled us to himself and gave us the ministry of reconciliation; [19]that is, in Christ God was reconciling the world to himself, not counting their trespasses against them, and entrusting to us the message of reconciliation. [20]Therefore, we are ambassadors for Christ, God making his appeal through us. We implore you on behalf of Christ, be reconciled to God. [21]For our sake he made him to be sin who knew no sin, so that in him we might become the righteousness of God.

"[1]Working together with him, then, we appeal to you not to receive the grace of God in vain."

_____

_____

_____


## 2.2 Group Discussion

1.  What is the mission of God?

_____

_____

_____


2.  How do you view the mission of God as it relates to you as an individual and us as a community?

_____

_____

_____


3.  In your own words, what is the difference between agreement and ownership?

_____

_____

4. How would you rate our ownership of the mission of God as a community?

_____

_____

_____

5. How can we encourage one another toward ownership?

_____

_____

_____

6. How does it make you feel to be invited into participation with God on his mission?

_____

_____

_____

7. In what ways do you see God stirring a holy discontentment in your heart?

_____

_____

_____

8. What are three things we can start doing this week as a community group to respond to the call of ownership?

_____

_____

_____

## 2.3 Prayer

- Thank God for the reconciling power of the gospel.
- Pray for the Holy Spirit to give us a heart for the mission of God.
- Pray that we would not receive the grace of God in vain.

## 2.4 Experience

This week we are going to start to get out of the living room. Plan an evening or afternoon when we can get together as a group and walk through the neighborhood. On our walk we will pray for opportunities to be salt and light to our neighbors. We are going to pray that barriers to the gospel would come down and that we would be ready to join God on mission.

## 2.5 Personal Reflection

What does it look like for you personally to own the mission of God as a disciple and ambassador of Jesus?

_____

_____

_____

_____

# SESSION 3:
# REDEFINING COMMUNITY

*From chapter 4 of* Community: Taking Your Small Group Off Life Support:

## NEW WINE SKINS

The past two weeks we've been uncovering why we do community groups: community is an expression of the gospel. At this point, we are now better prepared to ask *how* to do community groups.

"What are community groups in light of these convictions? At this point I want us to be able to clean the slate and rebuild our understanding of community groups on these principles and convictions. Our previous experiences in small groups can limit our imagination of what community can be. So let's dream for a minute that we never sat in that uncomfortable circle and answered icebreaker questions. How would we live in community if we started from scratch?"[1]

What would it look like to build a community

- from a sense of vision rather than reaction;
- with purpose rather than as a product;
- that sees community as who we are rather than what we do;
- that exists as a lifestyle rather than an event;
- that is life giving rather than life taking;
- that is a creative expression rather than conforming to a mold;
- that is a blessing to us as it was intended to be?

---

1  House, *Community,* 87.

## 3.1 Scripture Reflection

1 Peter 2:9–12: "⁹But you are a chosen race, a royal priesthood, a holy nation, a people for his own possession, that you may proclaim the excellencies of him who called you out of darkness into his marvelous light. ¹⁰Once you were not a people, but now you are God's people; once you had not received mercy, but now you have received mercy.

"¹¹Beloved, I urge you as sojourners and exiles to abstain from the passions of the flesh, which wage war against your soul. ¹²Keep your conduct among the Gentiles honorable, so that when they speak against you as evildoers, they may see your good deeds and glorify God on the day of visitation."

_____

_____

_____


## 3.2 Group Discussion

1.  In what ways have we been too easily pleased with mediocre community?

_____

_____

_____


2.  Take turns describing your picture of a life-giving community.

_____

_____

_____


3.  How can we incorporate some of these ideas into our community group?

_____

_____

_____

4. How does our community reflect the life of a disciple who finds his or her identity in Christ and expresses that identity through worship of God, community with one another, and mission to the lost? Where are we lacking?

_____

_____

_____

5. What does it mean to experience community as a lifestyle rather than an event?

_____

_____

_____

6. What element of community are we good at, and which ones do we struggle with? (Make a list.)

_____

_____

_____

_____

_____

_____

_____

_____

7. Why do you think we struggle with certain elements of community?

_____

_____

_____

8.  Work together to build a vision statement for this community. Why do we exist as a community?

_____

_____

_____

## 3.3 Prayer

- Pray that our hearts would be inclined toward each other, helping one another grow as disciples of Jesus.
- Pray that we would speak life-giving truth into the lives of one another.
- Pray for life-giving community.

## 3.4 Experience

This week we are going to start learning more about our neighborhood. Each member of the group will be sent to gather as much information as possible about the neighborhood and what is going on around us. We have two goals:

1.  Make a list of opportunities to engage with our neighbors by tracking down events and service opportunities at the local schools, community centers, neighborhood associations, neighborhood blogs, bulletin boards, etc.

_____

_____

_____

_____

_____

_____

_____

_____

_____

_____

2. Find natural gathering places for community within the neighborhood and describe what goes on there and why it has become a community hub.

_____

_____

_____

_____

_____

_____

_____

_____

_____

_____

## 3.5 Personal Reflection

What areas do you most want to see change in your community? How can you be a positive influence for that change?

_____

_____

_____

_____

_____

_____

_____

_____

_____

_____

# SESSION 4:
# NEIGHBORHOOD

*From chapter 5 of* Community: Taking Your Small Group Off Life Support:

## THE NEIGHBORHOOD APPROACH

"Much has been written over the last decade on the idea of *incarnational ministry*. God entered into history to redeem us from our rebellion and therefore we should, as his ambassadors, bring the gospel into culture rather than detach from it. *Incarnate* means to embody, typify, or represent. We are called to embody the gospel within the world.

"In John 17, Jesus tells us that he is sending us into the world even though we are not of this world. We have been given to Jesus by the Father, and now we get to proclaim his goodness to the world. This concept is anchored in our purpose to image God, and I am therefore all for incarnational ministry.

"The question is: What does incarnational church look like? The conversation on this subject has produced a variety of churches with diverse interpretations of what it means to be incarnational. I am convinced that it is more than edgy music and candles. Incarnational ministry will begin with the mobilization of the saints to embody the gospel in community. Jesus broke into our world, lived among us, and changed everything. That just makes Christian coffee shops seem trite. You cannot build a ministry that requires the world to come to it and call it incarnational. We have to go. We have to go into the world as ambassadors of Jesus.

"This conviction has inspired the vision for community groups within Mars Hill Church to mobilize the body for the advancement of the kingdom of God—to see the name of Jesus exalted in our city and yours through the proclamation of the Word and the incarnation of the gospel through community. Around this conviction we have built a missional strategy for reaching our city by building our groups around particular neighborhoods that have distinct cultures and people groups. Community groups are structured geographically around these neighborhoods and focus specific missional efforts on reaching these neighborhoods. We call this the neighborhood approach."[1]

1   House, *Community*, 105–106.

## 4.1 Scripture Reflection

John 17:10–26: "'¹⁰All mine are yours, and yours are mine, and I am glorified in them. ¹¹And I am no longer in the world, but they are in the world, and I am coming to you. Holy Father, keep them in your name, which you have given me, that they may be one, even as we are one. ¹²While I was with them, I kept them in your name, which you have given me. I have guarded them, and not one of them has been lost except the son of destruction, that the Scripture might be fulfilled. ¹³But now I am coming to you, and these things I speak in the world, that they may have my joy fulfilled in themselves. ¹⁴I have given them your word, and the world has hated them because they are not of the world, just as I am not of the world. ¹⁵I do not ask that you take them out of the world, but that you keep them from the evil one. ¹⁶They are not of the world, just as I am not of the world. ¹⁷Sanctify them in the truth; your word is truth. ¹⁸As you sent me into the world, so I have sent them into the world. ¹⁹And for their sake I consecrate myself, that they also may be sanctified in truth.

"'²⁰I do not ask for these only, but also for those who will believe in me through their word, ²¹that they may all be one, just as you, Father, are in me, and I in you, that they also may be in us, so that the world may believe that you have sent me. ²²The glory that you have given me I have given to them, that they may be one even as we are one, ²³I in them and you in me, that they may become perfectly one, so that the world may know that you sent me and loved them even as you loved me. ²⁴Father, I desire that they also, whom you have given me, may be with me where I am, to see my glory that you have given me because you loved me before the foundation of the world. ²⁵O righteous Father, even though the world does not know you, I know you, and these know that you have sent me. ²⁶I made known to them your name, and I will continue to make it known, that the love with which you have loved me may be in them, and I in them.'"

---

---

---

---

---

## 4.2 Group Discussion

1. How does seeing your neighborhood as a mission field make ownership more accessible?

_____

_____

_____

2. How do we interact with our neighbors today?

_____

_____

_____

3. Where is there a difference between God's heart for your neighbors and your own?

_____

_____

_____

4. What does it look like to repent of apathy, indifference, and fear of man when it comes to the salvation of our neighbors? (Refer to chapter 9.)

_____

_____

_____

5. How can we provide an alternative to the transience and isolation in our neighborhood?

_____

_____

_____

6.   What must we do to contextualize the gospel in this neighborhood?

_____

_____

_____

7.   Make a list of neighbors, friends, and coworkers whose eyes you are asking God to open to the truth of the gospel.

_____

_____

_____

_____

_____

_____

_____

_____

_____

## 4.3 Prayer

- Pray that the Holy Spirit would give us a heart for loving the lost in our neighborhood.
- Pray for opportunities to interact with our neighbors.
- Pray that God would use our community to bring our neighbors to meet Jesus.

## 4.4 Experience

This week we are going to do research. Our goal is to understand what our neighborhood values. Each member will be asked to have three conversations with a neighbor, barista, grocery clerk, mailman, community center coordinator, or any other person (not in your group or church) who has a pulse on the community. Bring your notes back to the group next week. Questions you could ask include:

- What do you think are the three highest values of this neighborhood?

_____

_____

_____

- What do you value most in life?

_____

_____

_____

- What are the biggest needs of this neighborhood?

_____

_____

_____

- How could a community of people serve this neighborhood?

_____

_____

_____

- Where does community happen in our neighborhood?

_____

_____

_____

- How do you personally experience community?

_____

_____

_____

- What do you love about this neighborhood?

_____

_____

_____

- What would you change about this neighborhood?

_____

_____

_____

## 4.5 Personal Reflection

Where is your heart when it comes to praying for your neighbors and opportunities to share the gospel? How is God challenging you in this area?

_____

_____

_____

_____

_____

_____

_____

# SESSION 5:
## SPACES

*From chapter 6 of* Community: Taking Your Small Group Off Life Support:

## VIEWING YOUR NEIGHBORHOOD AS SPACES

The goal of this lesson is for us to learn how to effectively engage with our neighborhood in ways that bless. "These spaces are how we belong to one another *and* how we engage with culture around us."[1]

## SPACES OF ENGAGEMENT

To help us understand these spaces in the context of community, we have identified four spaces in which your group should exist:

- Fellowship: Times to encourage one another in our lives with Jesus (most intimate).
- Hospitality: A safe place for anyone to belong to our communities.
- Service: Meeting the practical needs of our neighborhoods.
- Participation: Joining with our neighbors in common spaces and events (least intimate).

## BARRIERS AND BRIDGES

"As we identify barriers to the gospel, we can begin to build bridges to our neighbors. Bridges will look different in every context, but they start with a community of believers who have been changed by Jesus and want to share that joy with the world around them. A bridge is anything that provides an opportunity to your neighbors to be blessed and to experience the grace of God through your community."[2]

---

1    House, *Community*, 134.
2    Ibid., 130.

"As we open our eyes to the opportunities around us, we can begin to identify and dismantle barriers to the gospel. Expanding the spaces in which your group exists will increase their effectiveness for the gospel. Linking those spaces will make your community groups a kingdom force. This requires a new understanding of community groups as a vehicle for mission and kingdom. It requires us to be the church. It requires us to live a lifestyle of community.

"As you begin to pray about how your group can be more effective in reaching your neighborhood, consider what barriers exist and how existing in different spaces can help bridge those barriers. In the next chapter we will look at how that changes the day-to-day rhythms of community."[3]

---

3   Ibid., 145–146.

## 5.1 Scripture Reflection

Matthew 28:16–20: "[16]Now the eleven disciples went to Galilee, to the mountain to which Jesus had directed them. [17]And when they saw him they worshiped him, but some doubted. [18]And Jesus came and said to them, 'All authority in heaven and on earth has been given to me. [19]Go therefore and make disciples of all nations, baptizing them in the name of the Father and of the Son and of the Holy Spirit, [20]teaching them to observe all that I have commanded you. And behold, I am with you always, to the end of the age.'"

_____

_____

_____

## 5.2 Group Discussion

1. How are we engaging our neighbors individually and as a group?

_____

_____

_____

2. What internal obstacles are present in our group that inhibit us from being on mission?

_____

_____

_____

3. What are the barriers to the gospel in our neighborhood?

_____

_____

_____

4. How can we actively identify the barriers more clearly?

_____

_____

_____

5. Discuss how you can build bridges through the spaces of:
   a. Participation

_____

_____

_____

   b. Service

_____

_____

_____

   c. Hospitality

_____

_____

_____

   d. Fellowship

_____

_____

_____

6. Make a list of opportunities in each space and discuss how your group might look different if you trafficked in all four spaces.

_____

_____

_____

## 5.3 Prayer

- Pray for favor within our neighborhood.
- Pray that barriers to the gospel would be removed in our neighborhood.
- Pray that we would see our neighbors come to know Jesus.

## 5.4 Experience

It is time for some fun. Pick one of the natural places of community that you found in your research last week and plan an evening out with the group. Not everyone has to attend but do your best to make it. This is a time for us to relax and celebrate our friendships.

## 5.5 Personal Reflection

How will experiencing community in different spaces stretch you personally in being a disciple maker and setting your priorities?

_____

_____

_____

_____

# SESSION 6:
# RHYTHMS

*From chapter 7 of* Community: Taking Your Small Group Off Life Support:

## A NEW RHYTHM

"Breaking free from an event-focused view of community is not that easy. Most of our small group experiences have been event-based Bible studies or something similar. In order to break such patterns, we must begin by reimagining the basic rhythms of community.

"Rhythms can be defined as the when, where, and what of the community. For our discussion we will call them the *time*, *scene*, and *substance* of a community group. For example, the canonical event-based community group meets at 7:00 p.m. every Tuesday night (when/time), in the leader's living room (where/scene), for a Bible study (what/substance). This becomes the rhythm of the group. On Tuesdays we are a community, and the rest of the week we are living our lives individually.

"When these rhythms are rigid and finite, a community group will remain event based. Rigid group rhythms often produce inauthentic and labored groups. Challenging these rhythms is the beginning of reinventing your community group.

"I want leaders to constantly ask questions about why they do things. Why do we meet at this time? Why do we meet in this place? Why do we do this when we get together? Does this give life? As we ask these questions and realize that community can be more than once a week, we are on our way to living, breathing community groups.

"As we answer these questions, however, the goal is not simply to live life together more. The goal is to be inspired by the death and resurrection of Jesus to live differently. We want to offer more opportunities because we love our brothers and sisters and we have an urgency to share the love of Christ with our neighbors. Don't settle for a new system. If we want to effect change in the lives of our neighbors, we must be willing to be destroyed and rebuilt by the gospel. The questions of time, scene, and substance are questions about how we can be the gospel to one another in community."[1]

---

1  House, *Community*, 150.

## 6.1 Scripture Reflection

Acts 2:42–47: "⁴²And they devoted themselves to the apostles' teaching and the fellowship, to the breaking of bread and the prayers. ⁴³And awe came upon every soul, and many wonders and signs were being done through the apostles. ⁴⁴And all who believed were together and had all things in common. ⁴⁵And they were selling their possessions and belongings and distributing the proceeds to all, as any had need. ⁴⁶And day by day, attending the temple together and breaking bread in their homes, they received their food with glad and generous hearts, ⁴⁷praising God and having favor with all the people. And the Lord added to their number day by day those who were being saved."

_____

_____

_____

## 6.2 Group Discussion

I.  Make a list of all the things that the early church did in community in Acts 2. Is it possible for us to do all those things in two hours a week?

_____

_____

_____

_____

_____

_____

_____

_____

2.  What does it mean to develop a "culture of opportunity" within our community group?

_____

_____

_____

3. What ruts and expectations do you have that make it difficult to imagine new rhythms of community?

_____

_____

_____

4. Discuss how you could change the following rhythms to produce a more life-giving, Christ-honoring, mission-minded community group:

    a.   Time

_____

_____

_____

    b.   Scene

_____

_____

_____

    c.   Substance

_____

_____

_____

5. How do these rhythms line up with the people we are trying to reach in our neighborhood?

_____

_____

_____

6.  How do these rhythms interact with the spaces and opportunities that we discussed in the in the last session?

_____

_____

_____

7.  Complete the Group Plan outline as a group (see appendix 1).

## 6.3 Prayer

- Pray for a new vision of life-giving community.
- Pray for the plan we are putting together.
- Pray that our community would be a source of life for us and for the lost that God has called us to reach.

## 6.4 Experience

Our last experience together is going to be building a Group Plan based on the things we have learned over the past six weeks through our study and experiences in the neighborhood. You may do this during the week or at your next meeting. Fill out the Group Plan found in appendix 1 and have each member of the group pray through what God is calling us to be as a community of his disciples on mission.

## 6.5 Personal Reflection

Reflect on how you have been challenged over the past six weeks and how God is calling you to be a life-giving member to this community.

_____

_____

_____

_____

_____

# APPENDIX I:
## GROUP PLAN

## INFORMATION

Neighborhood Coach: _____

Leader: _____

Missiologist: _____

Administrator: _____

Host: _____

Social Coordinator: _____

## GOALS AND PROJECTIONS

Culture or people group focus: _____

_____

_____

Number of people that our group is praying will come to Christ this year through the group: _____

Names of people that our group is praying would come to know Christ this year through the group:

_____     _____

_____     _____

_____     _____

_____     _____

_____     _____

_____     _____

_____     _____

_____     _____

Number of groups we want to see replicated this year to reach more people in our neighborhoods: _____

## OPPORTUNITIES

Participation (building relationships): _____

_____

_____

_____

Service (loving the city): _____

_____

_____

_____

_____

Hospitality (invitation into community): _____

_____

_____

_____

_____

_____

Gospel Community (transformation through prayer, Bible study, confession, repentance, etc.): _____

_____

_____

_____

_____

_____

Does our group have an understanding of how natural rhythms (activities we participate in anyway) can become an important part of a missional community group? _____

_____

_____

_____

_____

_____

# APPENDIX II:
# NEIGHBORHOOD PLAN

## INFORMATION

Neighborhood: _____

Coach: _____

Number of groups in our neighborhood: _____

## RESOURCES

Locations of natural community: _____

_____

_____

_____

Service and event agencies: _____

_____

_____

_____

Local papers and newsletters: _____

_____

_____

_____

## GOALS

Vision for our neighborhood: _____

_____

_____

_____

_____

_____

How many people are we praying to see come to Christ through community groups in the next year? _____

Number of groups currently in our neighborhood: _____

Projected number of groups in:

      3 months: _____

      6 months: _____

      12 months: _____

How many apprentices or new leaders do we need in the next year?

_____

_____

_____

_____

# APPENDIX III: COMMUNITY GROUP REPLICATION PLAN

## INFORMATION

Community Group Coach: _____

Community Group Leader: _____

Apprentice: _____

Neighborhood: _____

## REPLICATION GOALS

1. Advance the gospel of Jesus Christ and plant more communities.

2. Produce more opportunities for people to see and experience the gospel.

3. Continue to create compassion for those who don't know Jesus or don't have community.

4. Grow as disciples and make disciples.

## REPLICATION VISION

How many people do we pray for? _____

When do we want to replicate to achieve the above goals? _____

_____

_____

_____

Who or what is our mission field? _____

_____

_____

Who are our potential apprentices?

_____     _____

_____     _____

Where are our potential host sites?

_____     _____

_____     _____

## STEPS FOR REPLICATION READINESS

1.  Identify Apprentice

2.  Vision for Group

3.  Core Group

4.  Host Location (mission before opportunity)

5.  Replication Timeline (This next section should include dates when the apprentice leads the group, a replication party, and a launch date.)

| Date | Event | Location |
|------|-------|----------|
|      |       |          |
|      |       |          |
|      |       |          |
|      |       |          |

# APPENDIX IV:
## COMMUNITY GROUP DIAGNOSTIC

**Date** _____

**Community Group Leader** _____

Please complete this Community Group Diagnostic (CGD) by filling in the bubble of the answer that best describes you or your community group. Please be thoughtful and accurate. This is not a question of pass or fail, but merely a diagnostic to assist our leaders and apprentices in training this next year.

### 1.1 Gospel Saturation

| | 0 | 1 | 2 | 3 | 4 |
|---|---|---|---|---|---|
| | Strongly Disagree | Disagree | Unsure | Agree | Strongly Agree |

1. We regularly discuss how the gospel is transforming us.
   - 0 Strongly Disagree ○ 1 Disagree ○ 2 Unsure ○ 3 Agree ○ 4 Strongly Agree ○

2. We regularly repent in front of one other.
   - 0 Strongly Disagree ○ 1 Disagree ○ 2 Unsure ○ 3 Agree ○ 4 Strongly Agree ○

3. We remind each other of the gospel naturally in conversation.
   - 0 Strongly Disagree ○ 1 Disagree ○ 2 Unsure ○ 3 Agree ○ 4 Strongly Agree ○

4. We are constantly brought back to the gospel when a problem arises.
   - 0 Strongly Disagree ○ 1 Disagree ○ 2 Unsure ○ 3 Agree ○ 4 Strongly Agree ○

5. We preach the gospel to one another and ourselves regularly.
   - 0 Strongly Disagree ○ 1 Disagree ○ 2 Unsure ○ 3 Agree ○ 4 Strongly Agree ○

## 1.2 Gospel Community

|  | 0 | 1 | 2 | 3 | 4 |
|---|---|---|---|---|---|

1. We regularly speak to one another outside of our CG night.

| Never | Rarely | Sometimes | Often | Always |
|---|---|---|---|---|
| ○ | ○ | ○ | ○ | ○ |

2. We regularly have people from CG over for dinner.

| Never | Rarely | Sometimes | Often | Always |
|---|---|---|---|---|
| ○ | ○ | ○ | ○ | ○ |

3. We naturally discuss God's Word through normal conversation.

| Never | Rarely | Sometimes | Often | Always |
|---|---|---|---|---|
| ○ | ○ | ○ | ○ | ○ |

4. We naturally speak of our struggles with one another.

| Never | Rarely | Sometimes | Often | Always |
|---|---|---|---|---|
| ○ | ○ | ○ | ○ | ○ |

5. We pray gospel-centered prayers (personally and for others).

| Never | Rarely | Sometimes | Often | Always |
|---|---|---|---|---|
| ○ | ○ | ○ | ○ | ○ |

## 1.3 Gospel Mission

|  | 0 | 1 | 2 | 3 | 4 |
|---|---|---|---|---|---|

1. We have a clearly defined missional agenda for our CG.

| Strongly Disagree | Disagree | Unsure | Agree | Strongly Agree |
|---|---|---|---|---|
| ○ | ○ | ○ | ○ | ○ |

2. We have a clearly defined mission field for our CG.

| Strongly Disagree | Disagree | Unsure | Agree | Strongly Agree |
|---|---|---|---|---|
| ○ | ○ | ○ | ○ | ○ |

3. We live in close proximity to those we are called to.

| Strongly Disagree | Disagree | Unsure | Agree | Strongly Agree |
|---|---|---|---|---|
| ○ | ○ | ○ | ○ | ○ |

4. We regularly spend time with those we are called to.

| Strongly Disagree | Disagree | Unsure | Agree | Strongly Agree |
|---|---|---|---|---|
| ○ | ○ | ○ | ○ | ○ |

5. We regularly involve non-Christians in our activities.

| Strongly Disagree | Disagree | Unsure | Agree | Strongly Agree |
|---|---|---|---|---|
| ○ | ○ | ○ | ○ | ○ |

## 1.4 Missional Frequency

| | 0 | 1 | 2 | 3 | 4 |
|---|---|---|---|---|---|

1. How well do you know the stories of your next-door neighbors?

| I don't | Not well | Somewhat | Pretty well | Very well |
|---|---|---|---|---|
| ○ | ○ | ○ | ○ | ○ |

2. How often do unbelievers spend time in your CG?

| Never | Rarely | 1/month | Weekly | 2+/week |
|---|---|---|---|---|
| ○ | ○ | ○ | ○ | ○ |

3. How often does your CG spend time with unbelievers on their territory where they feel comfortable?

| Never | Rarely | 1/month | Weekly | 2+/week |
|---|---|---|---|---|
| ○ | ○ | ○ | ○ | ○ |

4. How many people in your CG do your closest unbelieving friends know by name?

| None | One or two | Three or four | Five or six | Many |
|---|---|---|---|---|
| ○ | ○ | ○ | ○ | ○ |

5. Would you bring your closest unbelieving friends to a typical get-together of your CG?

| No | Depends on event | Yes, but haven't | Yes, I do sometimes | Yes, I do always |
|---|---|---|---|---|
| ○ | ○ | ○ | ○ | ○ |

---

## 2.1 Fellowship

| | 0 | 1 | 2 | 3 | 4 |
|---|---|---|---|---|---|

1. How well do you know each other's stories?

| I don't | Not well | Somewhat | Pretty well | Very well |
|---|---|---|---|---|
| ○ | ○ | ○ | ○ | ○ |

2. How fluent is your CG in speaking gospel instead of good advice?

| Not | Struggles | Somewhat fluent | Mostly fluent | Fluent |
|---|---|---|---|---|
| ○ | ○ | ○ | ○ | ○ |

3. How often do you talk with people in your CG about how God's Word is changing you?

| Never | Rarely | 1/month | Weekly | 2+/week |
|---|---|---|---|---|
| ○ | ○ | ○ | ○ | ○ |

4. How well do you listen to the needs of your CG?

| I don't | Not well | Somewhat | Pretty well | Very well |
|---|---|---|---|---|
| ○ | ○ | ○ | ○ | ○ |

5. How well do you intentionally listen to what God is saying to you through his Word?

| I don't | Not well | Somewhat | Pretty well | Very well |
|---|---|---|---|---|
| ○ | ○ | ○ | ○ | ○ |

## 2.2 Hospitality

| 0 | 1 | 2 | 3 | 4 |
|---|---|---|---|---|

1. How often do you have opportunities for non-believers to hang out with your CG?

| Never | 1/week | 2-3/week | 4-6/week | Nightly |
|---|---|---|---|---|
| ○ | ○ | ○ | ○ | ○ |

2. How often do you eat meals with those in your CG?

| Never | Rarely | 1/month | Weekly | 2+/week |
|---|---|---|---|---|
| ○ | ○ | ○ | ○ | ○ |

3. How often do you eat meals with non-believers?

| Never | Rarely | 1/month | Weekly | 2+/week |
|---|---|---|---|---|
| ○ | ○ | ○ | ○ | ○ |

4. How willing are you to eat meals with others spontaneously?

| Not willing | Maybe | Somewhat | Willing | Eager |
|---|---|---|---|---|
| ○ | ○ | ○ | ○ | ○ |

5. Do you see eating as an opportunity to create missional relationships?

| No | Not sure | Yes, but don't do it | Yes, infrequently | Yes, often |
|---|---|---|---|---|
| ○ | ○ | ○ | ○ | ○ |

## 2.3 Service

| 0 | 1 | 2 | 3 | 4 |
|---|---|---|---|---|

1. How often do you bless others in your CG in word, service, or gift?

| Never | Rarely | Occasionally | Often | Regularly |
|---|---|---|---|---|
| ○ | ○ | ○ | ○ | ○ |

2. How often do you bless others in your neighborhood in word, service, or gift?

| Never | Rarely | Occasionally | Often | Regularly |
|---|---|---|---|---|
| ○ | ○ | ○ | ○ | ○ |

3. How often do you meet the needs of others without being asked?

| Never | Rarely | Occasionally | Often | Regularly |
|---|---|---|---|---|
| ○ | ○ | ○ | ○ | ○ |

4. How willing are you to serve others without being asked?

| Unwilling | If pressured | Somewhat | Willing | Eager |
|---|---|---|---|---|
| ○ | ○ | ○ | ○ | ○ |

5. In which way does your CG bless others most/best?

| Speaking | Listening | Encouraging | Serving | Praying |
|---|---|---|---|---|
| ○ | ○ | ○ | ○ | ○ |

## 2.4 Participation

| 0 | 1 | 2 | 3 | 4 |
|---|---|---|---|---|

1. How often do you recreate with others in your CG?

| Never | Rarely | 1/month | Weekly | 2+/week |
|---|---|---|---|---|
| ○ | ○ | ○ | ○ | ○ |

2. How well do you know what events are happening in your neighborhood?

| I don't | Not very well | Somewhat | Pretty well | Very well |
|---|---|---|---|---|
| ○ | ○ | ○ | ○ | ○ |

3. How often does your CG participate in neighborhood events?

| Never | 1/quarter | 1/month | Weekly | Daily |
|---|---|---|---|---|
| ○ | ○ | ○ | ○ | ○ |

4. How often do you engage in conversation with non-believers in public spaces?

| Never | Rarely | 1/month | Weekly | 2+/week |
|---|---|---|---|---|
| ○ | ○ | ○ | ○ | ○ |

5. How many neighbors do you know by name?

| None | One or two | Three or four | Five or six | Many |
|---|---|---|---|---|
| ○ | ○ | ○ | ○ | ○ |

CPSIA information can be obtained at www.ICGtesting.com
Printed in the USA
BVOW082247170912

300557BV00003B/2/P